Happy Place

Happy Place

Pamela Mala Sinha

Happy Place
first published 2017 by
Scirocco Drama
An imprint of J. Gordon Shillingford Publishing Inc.

Scirocco Drama Editor: Glenda MacFarlane
Cover design by Terry Gallagher/Doowah Design Inc.
Author photo by Lori Dorn
Production photos by Cylla von Tiedemann

Printed and bound in Canada on 100% post-consumer recycled paper.

We acknowledge the financial support of the Manitoba Arts Council and The Canada Council for the Arts for our publishing program.

Library and Archives Canada Cataloguing in Publication

Sinha, Pamela Mala, author
Happy place / Pamela Mala Sinha.

A play.
ISBN 978-1-927922-13-2 (paperback)

I. Title.

PS8637.I633H36 2016 C812'.6 C2016-905183-8

J. Gordon Shillingford Publishing
P.O. Box 86, RPO Corydon Avenue, Winnipeg, MB Canada R3M 3S3

For

Damon D'Oliveira

and

Brian Scott

Pamela Mala Sinha

Pamela Mala Sinha is an award-winning Canadian actress and playwright. Selected theatre credits include *Happy Place* (Soulpepper), *Nirbhaya* (Assembly Theatre / UK, NY), and *The Little Years* (Stratford Production / Tarragon Theatre). Selected TV / Film: three seasons on *ER* (NBC), *Huff* (HBO), *Traders, Live from Baghdad, Breakaway,* and *What We Have.*

Pamela was the recipient of Canada's prestigious Dora Mavor Moore Awards for Outstanding New Play and Outstanding Lead Actress for her solo debut play, *Crash* (Scirocco Drama), also included in Bloomsbury's (UK) anthology *Audition Speeches for Black, South Asian and Middle Eastern Actors. Crash* toured to New York with Soulpepper Theatre in July 2017, and will continue touring internationally through 2018. Pamela's new commission with Soulpepper, *New,* is a play inspired by her parents' immigration to Canada and their coming of age. Pamela is in development on the feature film adaptation of *Happy Place* with Sienna Films and director Helen Shaver, slated for production in early 2018.

Acknowledgements

I am deeply grateful to a number of individuals who have supported me during the development of this play: Iris Turcott (Factory Crosscurrents) and Bob White (Stratford Festival) for producing the first public reading; Guillermo Verdecchia for his dramaturgical insights; director Alan Dilworth for his always-invaluable notes in rehearsal; and to those actresses whose brilliant work inspired me to write these parts: Catherine Fitch, Kristen Thomson, Liisa Repo-Martell and Maria Vacratsis.

I am indebted to Soulpepper Theatre Company; not only for premiering *Happy Place*, but for their continued belief in and support of my work.

Finally, to my family, immediate and extended...your love propels me in this life.

Production History

Happy Place had its world premiere at Toronto's Soulpepper Theatre in September, 2015 with the following cast:

SAMIRA .... Oyin Oladejo
MILDRED .... Diane D'Aquila
CELINE .... Pamela Mala Sinha
NINA .... Liisa Repo-Martell
JOYCE .... Caroline Gillis
ROSEMARY .... Irene Poole
LOUISE .... Deborah Drakeford

Directed by Alan Dilworth
Set Design by Lorenzo Savoini
Lighting Design by Kimberly Purtell
Original Music and Sound Design by Debashis Sinha
Costume Design by Ken MacKenzie

Happy Place was presented by Touchstone Theatre in association with Ruby Slippers Theatre in October, 2017 at The Firehall Arts Centre, Vancouver, with the following cast:

SAMIRA .... Adele Noronha
MILDRED.................... Nicola Cavendish
CELINE............................ Sereana Malani
NINA......................................Laara Sadiq
JOYCE.................................. Diane Brown
ROSEMARY / KRISTA... Colleen Wheeler
LOUISE........................Donna Yamamoto

Directed by Roy Surette
Set Design by Pam Johnson
Lighting Design by Adrian Muir
Costume Design by Christine Reimer
Original Music and Sound Design by Dorothy Dittrich

Mildred (Diane D'Aquila) breaks down in front of Rosemary (Irene Poole).

Joyce (Caroline Gillis), Rosemary (Irene Poole) and Celine (Pamela Mala Sinha) in the aftermath of Mildred's breakdown.

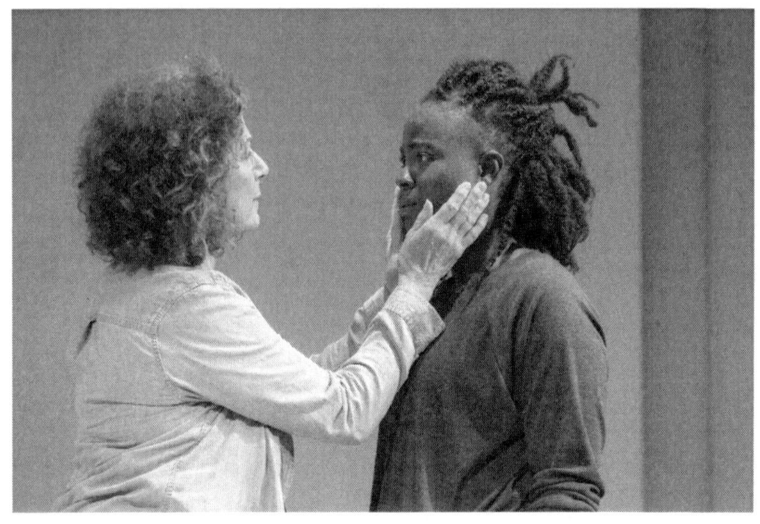

Mildred says goodbye to Samira (Oyin Oladejo).

Nina (Liisa Repo-Martell) responds to the results of her sonogram presented by her therapist, Louise (Deborah Drakeford).

Production Notes

The action of the play takes place in the interior of an in-patient care facility and its enclosed courtyard.

The individual rooms of all the women are simply indicated as "Bedroom." There is a door that leads to a bathroom offstage.

A hallway opens onto the "Common Room," which has a pay phone at one end, and a kitchen counter with a kettle and small fridge at the other. There is a couch, and a long table with benches on either side of this room.

Suggestions: The area of the long table in the Common Room may double as the "Cafeteria" and/or "Louise's Office." Similarly, the Common Room could transform into the "Courtyard," with the couch doubling as the park bench.

Please note: slashes within lines indicate the point at which the following character begins speaking OVER the lines of the previous character (who *continues* speaking their text.)

Any text written side by side indicates characters speaking at the same time.

Cast of Characters

SAMIRA .... twenties

MILDRED .... sixties

CELINE .... late thirties

NINA ....late forties

JOYCE .... fifties

ROSEMARY .... forties

LOUISE .... fifties

KRISTA... a nurse
(can be doubled by the actor playing ROSEMARY)

ACT I

Scene One

Bedroom.

A young woman, SAMIRA, stands at the end of a bed. KRISTA, a nurse, but not dressed like a nurse, has in her arms a blow dryer, curling iron, and a bag of razors.

On her way out, her eye catches SAMIRA pulling a tampon from her bag.

KRISTA: *(Reaching for the tampon.)* Oh—I'll have to take that.

SAMIRA: What…*this?*

KRISTA: Just go on over to the nurses' station—Ivan will give you a pad.

SAMIRA: *(Pulling it away.)* Wait—I don't get it—you think…what? I mean, what would I do with it—like, stuff it down my throat, or…?

KRISTA takes the tampon and leaves.

(At the door, calling after her.) Well—you know what? Hey, Krista—know what? Even if I *did* want to stuff it down my throat… All you'd have to do is pull the goddamn string.

Scene Two

Hallway. Afternoon.

CELINE, late thirties, stands against a door, listening. She has an easy elegance; tasteful make-up, expensive robe.

MILDRED, sixties, in head-to-toe polyester, passes her — then realizes what she's up to.

MILDRED: Who's in there?

CELINE: New girl.

MILDRED: Oh yeah. Met her.

CELINE: *(Surprised.)* When'd she get here?

MILDRED: Couple of days ago.

MILDRED joins her at the door.

(Beat, listening.) She's laughing.

CELINE: No, she's not.

MILDRED: She's laughing!

CELINE: Who—Dr. Stratton?

MILDRED: New girl.

Suddenly LOUISE (Dr. Stratton), fifties, very fashionable and a little shaken, opens the door. SAMIRA emerges, looking perfectly fine.

CELINE:	Hi!	MILDRED:	*(Taking in LOUISE.)* We're going to dinner. Fish and chips!

LOUISE: That the special today? Sounds wonderful. Enjoy, ladies.

She disappears into her office, shutting the door behind her.

MILDRED: *(To SAMIRA.)* What did you say to her?

CELINE: *(To SAMIRA.)* She's not really asking.

SAMIRA smiles briefly, then walks towards her room.

Aren't you coming?

SAMIRA: I'm a little tired. Jet lag.

MILDRED: I'm Mildred. She's Celine.

SAMIRA: Samira. *(Beat.)* Nice meeting you.

The two women watch her continue down the hallway.

MILDRED: *(Beat.)* I say slasher.

CELINE: Nope. Wrists were clean.

MILDRED: Jeez you're fast. Bipolar for sure.

CELINE: Why?

MILDRED: Too normal. *(Mischievously.)* Could be fun.

Scene Three

Common Room.

NINA, late forties, thin, pretty, is standing in front of the TV; a Lifetime *movie plays. She sits on the couch, watches for a bit, then presses the volume on the remote. It doesn't work.*

LOUISE, carrying a stack of magazines, passes the open doors on her way to SAMIRA's bedroom.

LOUISE *(Offstage):* We talked about this.

Beat.

SAMIRA *(Offstage):* I'm writing in my journal. You told me to.

LOUISE *(Offstage):* You can write out here.

SAMIRA *(Offstage):* No I can't.

NINA gets up and manually turns the TV volume off.

LOUISE *(Offstage):* I'll sign you out for the courtyard if you like. It's beautiful outside.

SAMIRA *(Offstage):* I'm happy here.

LOUISE *(Offstage):* You need to spend some time outside your room.

LOUISE, moving away from her bedroom, can be seen in the hallway by NINA.

LOUISE: There's no need for this, Samira. Come on now.

Pause.

Then SAMIRA comes charging through the doors of the Common Room.

SAMIRA: Well now I'm not going to write!

SAMIRA throws herself on the opposite end of the couch from NINA, who continues to watch the muted TV. LOUISE, satisfied, leaves.

Beat.

(To NINA.) Is it broken?

NINA: *(Not looking at her.)* What?

SAMIRA: The TV.

NINA: No.

KRISTA enters with a clipboard, sees them, then leaves.

SAMIRA: Why are they always coming in all the time?! Even when my door is closed.

NINA: It's not supposed to be closed. *(She looks at SAMIRA for the first time.)* Ever. *(She looks away again.)* Spot checks.

SAMIRA: What?

NINA: Checking what you're up to—on the spot. And that you're still alive. Not everybody's here for the same thing, but that for sure is the same. We should be dead.

Beat.

SAMIRA: My friend said if I really wanted to kill myself, why didn't I jump off a building.

NINA: Good point. Just kidding.

NINA suddenly laughs.

They don't want us to do it again, but every time they do one of those… *(Gesturing at the door.)* It just reminds us how much we wanted to do it in the first place!

CELINE enters and heads for the fridge — in her own world. JOYCE, fifties, follows, in an oversized kaftan and very made-up.

(To SAMIRA.) I'm sorry you're here but I'm glad you're here.

SAMIRA:	Thanks.	NINA:	*(Looking over at JOYCE.)* Joyce said that to me when I first got here. Now you can say it to the next person.

They go back to watching TV. CELINE leaves with her bottle of water. JOYCE — checking first to make sure CELINE is far enough down the hall — rushes over to NINA and SAMIRA.

JOYCE: Celine's mom tried to kill her!

SAMIRA: What?

NINA continues watching TV.

JOYCE: *(Pleased at SAMIRA's reaction.)* She sealed the windows and doors and turned on the gas but when the cat took off her mom ran out yelling, "there's no way no WAY we're going to heaven without Funny Bunny, Celine!" And then the cops showed up.

SAMIRA: Oh my god.

JOYCE: I know, eh?! *(Beat. At the TV.)* Why's the sound off?

Joyce picks up the remote.

NINA: *(To JOYCE.)* It doesn't work still.

SAMIRA: *(To JOYCE.)* Is she okay?

JOYCE: *(Turning up the volume manually.)* Who?

SAMIRA: Celine.

JOYCE: *(Confused by the question.)* Yeah.

NINA clocks SAMIRA's confusion.

NINA: Celine didn't just remember that stuff now. Joyce just found out about it. It's not new or anything. *(Beat.)* She also didn't tell her that.

JOYCE: We get each other.

NINA: *(To SAMIRA.)* No they don't.

Scene Four

Bedroom. Midnight.

SAMIRA is sitting bolt upright in bed. LOUISE *— chart in hand — peeks in for a spot check.*

LOUISE: Hey…what are you doing up? *(Beat.)* Samira?

Pause.

SAMIRA: There was a ring.

LOUISE: A ring?

SAMIRA: A wedding ring. *(Beat.)* It cut me. Inside.

LOUISE: *(Beat.)* Something did.

SAMIRA: How could a wedding ring cut?

LOUISE: A diamond, maybe.

Beat.

SAMIRA: I remembered it.

LOUISE: Okay.

SAMIRA: I just can't remember if I saw it or felt it.

Pause.

LOUISE: Traumatic memory is…indirect. The missing parts…the parts you can't remember—will come in / their own time.

SAMIRA: Pieces.

LOUISE: It's your mind's way of protecting you from having to face the pain all at once. The pieces are a good thing.

Pause.

SAMIRA: I want to go home.

LOUISE: Why do you want /to go home?

SAMIRA: I hate it here. My parents are paying a thousand dollars a DAY for me to be somewhere I hate.

LOUISE: Why do you hate it?

SAMIRA: I had a great childhood. I love my family. My family loves me. I have the two best friends in the world. I'm not like the people here.

LOUISE: You tried to kill yourself.

SAMIRA: So?

LOUISE: So did they.

SAMIRA: Not because I'm crazy. *(She lies down.)* I want to cut my head off. I want to cut it out of my head.

LOUISE: *(Softly.)* Cut what out?

SAMIRA: What I can't remember.

Scene Five

Common Room. Morning.

MILDRED sits alone at the table. SAMIRA enters, exhausted, and sits across from her.

LOUISE enters, surprised to see them there.

LOUISE: You ladies know you're early, right?

MILDRED: We're not early. We're bored.

Unlocking a cupboard, LOUISE loads something into the CD player, then locks it again. She exits. After a moment, Yo-Yo Ma's Bach Cello Suites begins to play.

SAMIRA: Why does she lock up the music?

MILDRED: *(Bored.)* We might slit our throats with a CD. *(Beat.)* How old are you?

SAMIRA: Twenty-four.

MILDRED: You look six. What do you do out there?

Beat.

SAMIRA: I'm an actor.

MILDRED: Really? Like on TV?!

LOUISE enters again; the women instantly fall silent. She places a large, beautiful basket of stones on the table.

(To LOUISE.) We gonna stone ourselves to death?

Ignoring her, LOUISE puts two small pots of gold and silver paint down next to the basket. CELINE and JOYCE enter and sit.

LOUISE: Hello, ladies! Where's Nina?

JOYCE: Check-up.

LOUISE: Right. Before we start, I thought we should talk about the changes for Group. Starting/ tomorrow

CELINE: We can't talk about something no one's bothered to tell us about.

LOUISE: You're right, Celine. *(Beat.)* The Psych team feels that smaller numbers in Group would be a better complement to your individual therapy. So from today, you ladies will form one group, and the other half of the ward/ will form

CELINE: So we're not actually talking about anything then. You've already decided.

SAMIRA: I still see Dr. Henderson?

LOUISE: *(To all of them.)* I'll keep working with all of your individual therapists as needed, and continue on as your Floor Counsellor.

JOYCE: *(Clapping quietly.)* Yay…

LOUISE: Nothing changes except/ for

JOYCE: Morning Group!

LOUISE: The size of Morning Group. Okay, Celine? *(Beat.)* For today, I'd like /everyone to—

NINA rushes in and sits beside MILDRED —

Everything okay, Nina?

— who immediately switches to a seat furthest away.

NINA: Peachy keeny!

LOUISE: I'd like everyone to pick out one stone from the basket.

The women reach into the basket at once. CELINE *waits.*

Take your time finding the right one... You'll be using it today to create your very own "memory" stone.

MILDRED: *(Picking one out.)* Call it what you want. I know a pet rock when I see one.

Scene Six

Bedroom.

SAMIRA sits cross-legged on her bed, journal unopened in front of her. NINA appears in the doorway, eating yogurt.

NINA: Hi.

SAMIRA: *(Surprised.)* Oh. Hi.

NINA: We watched TV together already so now I'm visiting you.

NINA scrapes the last of her yogurt.

SAMIRA: You like yogurt.

NINA: I need calcium. I'm eating for two.

SAMIRA: Oh—wow. When are you/ due?

NINA: What are your top ten names?

SAMIRA: For what?

NINA: A girl.

SAMIRA: I never thought about it.

NINA: You should start.

SAMIRA picks up her journal, and opens it.

Have you figured it out yet?

SAMIRA: What?

NINA: Why I'm here.

SAMIRA: I'm not trying to.

NINA: Yes, you are so.

Glancing down the hall, NINA steps into the room.

(In a hushed voice.) First they'll say something about them; like something you do or say that's just like them. But you're not. They're fishing. Joyce does it all the time here. Celine started doing it too but I think that's because she's here not because she does it in real life.

SAMIRA: *(Getting up.)* I need to finish journaling before bed.

NINA: They want to know. They're dying to know.

SAMIRA: See you later.

NINA watches her go.

NINA: How can you finish something you don't have?

SAMIRA: *(Offstage.)* What?

NINA: *(Pointing at the journal on the bed.)* You don't have it. So how can you finish it?

SAMIRA comes back; NINA grabs the journal.

What are you writing about?

SAMIRA: Can I have it please?

NINA: *(Keeping it from her.)* Writingwritingwriting.

SAMIRA: Give it to me and I'll tell you.

NINA: Only if you think about it, okay?

SAMIRA: Okay!

NINA: *(Testing her.)* Think about what?

SAMIRA: Nina, I want my journal!

NINA: Your top ten names. Not five. TEN.

NINA hands the book to SAMIRA, who grabs it and moves as far away from NINA as she can; NINA clocks this. She is suddenly very upset.

I only know the names I know. I can't pick from just only those—I'm not mean!

As soon as she leaves, SAMIRA sits heavily on the bed.

Scene Seven

Common Room.

SAMIRA, in pajamas hunched on a chair, is at the pay phone. CELINE waits for the kettle to boil in the kitchen area, trying to give her some privacy.

SAMIRA: *(Loud whisper, into the phone.)* I don't want you to visit I want you to send me a ticket! *(Beat.)* Is Daddy there—can I talk to him? *(Beat.)* Daddy? NO—because I just want to come home! *(Beat, crying.)* There's no one like me here.

KRISTA sticks her head in.

KRISTA: *(To SAMIRA.)* It's past nine, Samira, you know/ the rules…

SAMIRA: *(Into the phone.)* See?! They won't even let me talk to you here! *(Beat.)* Okay…yes. Okay. *(Beat.)* Bye.

She hangs up. Satisfied, KRISTA leaves.

SAMIRA remains where she is. The kettle boils. CELINE switches it off.

CELINE: I wanted to go home at first. But I'm glad I stayed.

SAMIRA: *(Beat.)* Why?

CELINE: Because when you laugh here, no one thinks you're feeling better.

Pause.

You're not the only one.

SAMIRA: The only what?

CELINE: *(Beat.)* He was the youth counsellor in my group home. I was twelve when he—

CELINE waits for SAMIRA to respond. She doesn't.

Because he was a—government worker, it was a big deal when it happened. I got sent to a fancy boarding school. I had a great teacher there—I made the honour roll every year because of him. Before graduation he applied to a bunch of Ivy League schools without telling me. He wanted to surprise me if I got into one.

SAMIRA: Did you?

CELINE: Harvard. So I asked him to be the one to drive me to the train station. On the way there he raped me.

Pause.

SAMIRA: Five years ago. My legs still shake at night.

CELINE: Every night?

SAMIRA: Only when they need to know…that they're free.

SAMIRA looks directly at CELINE, who looks back unflinchingly.

Did you tell them? When you got to Harvard?

CELINE: *(Beat.)* I never got off the train.

JOYCE, standing outside the open doors of the Common Room, has heard every word.

Scene Eight

Common Room.

JOYCE stands at the window. CELINE enters. Seeing her, Joyce starts waving enthusiastically at someone outside.

CELINE heads for the phone, picks up the receiver, and then hesitates.

JOYCE: *(Observing her.)* Are you calling Mohammed? Bill just left. Did you see us? We were outside.

CELINE begins punching in a long calling card number.

It's probably traffic. Bill always gives it an extra hour on Family Day. I think our husbands would really hit it off even if Mohammed is a Musli— but it's not like he wears one of those white hats or anything, so how would Bill even know, really, except I guess his name would kind of give/ it away…

CELINE: Hi, honey! *(It's the machine.)* …Oh. *(Beat.)* Hi, it's me. *(Beat.)* It's Sunday… *(Beat.)* I called last night but you didn't pick up. Was the ringer off? Your cell was off too, Mohammed, so if something happened how would anyone—*(She changes her tone.)* Maybe Adam was sleeping… Okay. Well. Let's talk tomorrow. *(Beat.)* Sorry I got upset about the phone. I love you. *(She tries to hang up but can't help herself.)* I just thought you guys were coming today that's all. *(She hangs up quickly.)* *Shit.*

Pause.

CELINE notices JOYCE staring.

He's a doctor. He's under a lot of stress right now.

JOYCE: Oh—I know! Bill's stress levels are so high he's not even supposed to be on the freeway but I just can't get him not to come.

CELINE looks at her a moment, then takes a seat at the table.

LOUISE enters; dropping off a stack of magazines on the table, she exits again.

SAMIRA enters with MILDRED; both take their seats at the table. MILDRED halfheartedly picks out a magazine and flips through it, stopping at a glossy car ad.

MILDRED: I need to get me one of those.

SAMIRA: *(Looking.)* A Porsche? Aren't they like, sixty thousand dollars?

MILDRED: *(Lightly.)* I got sixty thousand dollars.

LOUISE enters again, carrying a cheerful cardboard box and two small baskets — one with scissors, the other with glue sticks — which she places in front of MILDRED. MILDRED picks a pair of scissors out of the basket.

(Waving the scissors at LOUISE.) You don't think this is a bad idea?

LOUISE takes them from her.

JOYCE and NINA enter and take their seats. As LOUISE places a sheet of paper in front of each of them:

LOUISE: Because you've been working on deep relaxation in 'Health and Wellness' class, I thought for today we could make a collage of the place you would most like to visualize in your practice. What I like to call your "happy place."

MILDRED: That would be under a good man with fast hands.

Everyone but CELINE and SAMIRA laughs.

LOUISE: *(Amused.)* Sorry I can't help you with that, Mildred…

She pulls handfuls of magazine cutouts from the box.

I've selected some images here to start you off: here's some of the Grand Canyon, Niagara Falls, Victoria Falls, / the Nile

JOYCE: *(To everyone.)* Because water can be very soothing.

The women look less than enthusiastic.

LOUISE: Try and give this a chance. You can use them or not—it's entirely up to you.

She places a handful of cutouts in front of MILDRED.

MILDRED: *(Picking up a fistful.)* You cut all these out yourself?

LOUISE: I did!

MILDRED: You didn't have anything better to do?

LOUISE: *(Beat.)* If you don't see anything from what I've picked out, here are some Nature and Travel magazines. If you see something you like, go ahead and cut / it out

NINA: Are we supposed to cover the whole page?

LOUISE: There's no right or wrong way to do this, Nina—this is your visualization collage. Cut and paste as little—or as much—as you want. As long as the image inspires in you a sense of calm. Mountains maybe…? A bird, or / the ocean

JOYCE: *(Flipping through a magazine.)* Cottage furniture?

The women react.

Cottage furniture makes me calm.

LOUISE: I'd prefer if you found something in nature, Joyce.

CELINE: So there is a wrong way then.

LOUISE: Cottage furniture is fine.

Each in their own time, they begin cutting and gluing, except CELINE. MILDRED struggles with her scissors.

They're childproof, Mildred—they take getting used to. *(LOUISE demonstrates.)* See?

MILDRED tries again, unsuccessfully.

You'll get the hang of it. Okay, ladies—I'll be back!

The women work quietly for a few moments. Eventually MILDRED notices JOYCE trying not to stare at her.

MILDRED: *(Not looking up.)* Quit it.

JOYCE does – until she looks again.

Quit it, I said.

SAMIRA: Quit what?

MILDRED: *(To JOYCE.)* Staring at me all the time! *(Explaining to SAMIRA, pointing at her eyes.)* One's green and one's blue, eh? Old man's a German mutt, old lady's quarter Cherokee. Got an eyeball from each of 'em.

SAMIRA:	Heterochromia iridium.	MILDRED:	*(Continuing, catching JOYCE staring again.)* For Chrissakes!

NINA: *(To SAMIRA.)* What?

SAMIRA:	*(To NINA.)* Different coloured eyes.	MILDRED:	*(Sticking her face right in JOYCE's.)* You wanna look—SO LOOK!

NINA: *(Touching her stomach.)* What are the odds of that?

JOYCE tries to paste around MILDRED, who is in her way.

JOYCE: *(To MILDRED.)* Both my parents were part Indian.

MILDRED:	*(Her face in JOYCE's.)* *Both.* Really.	NINA:	*(To SAMIRA.)* No—really—what are the odds of that?

JOYCE: I'm part Sioux. You can't tell.

MILDRED: No. You can't.

SAMIRA: *(To MILDRED.)* I think your eyes are beautiful.

MILDRED: I think maybe it's some kinda curse. I could be doing the sex OLYMPICS for 'em every night when BAM—they can't get it up. Not if they're looking at me, anyway. They can do it doggie style, though. They usually take off a couple of weeks later.

JOYCE: *(Beat.)* Is that why you're here?

MILDRED: (*Back to her cutting.*) A Javex chaser is why I'm here, Joyce. How 'bout you?

JOYCE goes pale. LOUISE enters with a paper cup of coffee.

LOUISE: How are we doing, ladies?

MILDRED: WE are hating these scissors, Louise—these goddamn scissors make me wanna kill myself!

LOUISE notices CELINE hasn't moved.

LOUISE: Nothing here you like, Celine?

CELINE: I hate the woods.

LOUISE: You hate the woods?

CELINE: I'm allergic.

JOYCE: I'm allergic to the woods/ too, Louise—

LOUISE: Let's see if there isn't/ something here you

CELINE: There isn't.

JOYCE: *(Continuing.)*—and mosquitoes/ and blackflies too—

LOUISE: *(Going through CELINE's pile.)* Give me a second/ Joyce

JOYCE: *(Continuing.)*—so I don't think the woods are a very "happy" /place for me either so…

MILDRED: *(To LOUISE, looking at JOYCE.)* JEEZUZ would you please just shut her up!

CELINE: Can I go/ to my room?

JOYCE: Can I go too, Louise?

LOUISE: No Joyce—how about/ this one?

CELINE: It's not there.

LOUISE: This is /lovely?

CELINE: It's not in there…

JOYCE: This isn't working/ for me either, so…

LOUISE: Look at this / one!

CELINE: IT'S NOT IN THERE I SAID.

Everyone stops, shocked.

My baby's face. It's not in there.

Scene Nine

Bedroom. Night.

SAMIRA sits on the floor inside CELINE's doorway. It is very dark; the only light comes from the hallway.

SAMIRA: The phone was ringing. I was staring down at the last row of pills on the floor. The floor was hardwood, but deep, scratched hardwood from too many years of cheap student furniture. The pills kept falling into the grooves—I kept trying to line them up but they kept falling in. It was important that they line up…

She looks into the room at CELINE in bed, listening.

I can't remember why. *(Beat.)* I could only see the outlines of things—my hand, my knees on the floor, the bottles, the corners of the room…like when you burn the edges of a photograph—that's how it looked. I picked up the phone because I knew it was her, calling to say good night. While she was talking I thought, if her voice doesn't stop me, nothing will. That's when she said, "Love you." She always said that when she hung up with us but this time, after she said it she said, "You know I love you, right?" She never said that before. You know I love you, right? I thought if I do this, she'll think it's because I don't know she loves me. She'll think I wouldn't have done it if I knew she loved me. She'll think it's her fault. And you know what I thought next? I don't care. I'm dead already. And not even Mummy can keep me here.

Scene Ten

Common Room. Evening.

CELINE is on the floor, mid-game of Scrabble. SAMIRA, on the couch, plays too. MILDRED paces in the background, clearly not playing.

The remaining tiles are spread face down in the lid of the box JOYCE has balanced on her outstretched legs.

JOYCE: *(Writing her score.)* Fourteen. *(The pencil tip breaks.)* Shit!

CELINE: Stop pressing down so hard!

JOYCE: I can't help it—I get excited!

MILDRED: God this game is boring.

JOYCE tries to write.

CELINE: Give it here.

JOYCE does.

JOYCE: *(Casually.)* We should have invited that new girl to play.

SAMIRA: Who's new?

NINA enters.

JOYCE: She arrived this morning. They're putting her in our group.

NINA: If I have to pee one more time…

As NINA lies on the other end of the couch from SAMIRA:

CELINE: *(To JOYCE.)* What's she like?

JOYCE: *Rich.*

NINA: *(To JOYCE.)* What did you get?

JOYCE:	Twenty-six. *(Beat.)* I'm going to have to start sleeping on my stomach. My back is killing me.	CELINE:	*(Handing JOYCE the pencil.)* Double letter score.

NINA: *(Rubbing her belly.)* I can't sleep on my stomach anymore.

JOYCE: *(Writing the score.)* Is Ivan at the desk today?

CELINE: *(Playing her word.)* No one that good-looking has a right to live.

JOYCE: Maybe he'll give me something.

MILDRED: He'll give you something all right.

Suddenly MILDRED is hit with a sharp pain. She hides it.

CELINE: *(Counting her score.)* Twelve, no bonuses. Jesus.

NINA: I need a little lie-down.

JOYCE: *(Writing CELINE's score.)* You *are* lying down.

NINA stands.

Nina!

NINA: Okay. But I need more letters. *(To JOYCE.)* Can you pass me four tiles, please?

MILDRED: Bend down and get them yourself.

CELINE: *(To MILDRED.)* You're not even playing.

Avoiding MILDRED's gaze, JOYCE hands NINA four tiles.

SAMIRA: *(Placing her tiles.)* Best I can do.

CELINE: *(Looking at SAMIRA's word.)* That's just sad.

SAMIRA laughs.

NINA: *(Looking at her tiles, singsong-y.)* I really think it's time for a little lie-down…

JOYCE: Samira, seven points, no bonuses.

MILDRED: *(To NINA.)* You're a faker.

CELINE: Go Nina.

MILDRED: She's a faker.

CELINE: Nina—play your word.

MILDRED: She should be in a nuthouse, not here.

NINA: *(Suddenly standing.)* "I will not let anyone walk through my mind with their dirty feet." By Mahatma Gandhi.

She leaves.

MILDRED: Like I said…nuthouse.

CELINE: She's depressed. Very, very depressed.

MILDRED: Who isn't here?!

JOYCE: I was pregnant once.

MILDRED: Don't tell me—TWINS, right?

JOYCE: I miscarried, actually.

MILDRED: Both at once, or one at a time?

SAMIRA: I don't want to play anymore.

CELINE: Me either.

SAMIRA starts packing up the game; JOYCE helps. No one speaks.

(Finally, to MILDRED.) Why does she bug you so much?!

MILDRED: She shouldn't be here!

JOYCE: Can we please not fight?

CELINE: I'm not fighting. *(To MILDRED.)* I really want to know why you think that.

MILDRED: It's all in her head!

SAMIRA: It's all in my head too.

MILDRED: But you're not walking around pretending to be /pregnant

CELINE: You think she's pretending.

MILDRED: Nothing happened to her for Chrissakes, Celine—it's not real/ she's fuckin' nuts!

JOYCE: It's real to her.

MILDRED: NO—REAL's carrying around your own shit for a year—your own shit—don't tell me what's real I KNOW WHAT—

MILDRED suddenly stops—blank. She walks out.

SAMIRA: *(Beat, to CELINE.)* What does she mean... carry/...?

CELINE: She went in for a hysterectomy but the doctor's knife slipped. He was drunk.

SAMIRA:	Oh my god.	CELINE:	*(Continuing.)* She ended up with a colostomy. Had a bag for a year.

SAMIRA: Did she sue?

CELINE: I didn't ask.

JOYCE: *(Beat.)* They settled for close to a million. She drank the bleach the day she got the cheque.

Pause.

CELINE: *(Upset.)* I'm going to bed.

CELINE leaves.

JOYCE: Do you think it's true what Mildred said? That nothing happened to Nina?

SAMIRA: No. *(Beat.)* Something happened.

JOYCE continues packing up as SAMIRA watches — not really there.

Blackout.

Scene Eleven

Bedroom. Midnight.

Lights flash over SAMIRA who, sitting upright in bed, listens to the sound of a car in motion. Her eyes dart to the window…remembering…

SAMIRA: *(Whispering.)* I can manage from here…

She looks at a shaft of light spilling from the hallway into the path of her half-open door.

Pause.

A suspended moment…then flying out of bed she runs out of her room —

Krista! *(Offstage.)* KRISTA!

Scene Twelve

LOUISE's office. 2:00 AM.

LOUISE watches as SAMIRA, filled with nervous energy, speaks on the phone with the police.

SAMIRA: I can't remember the name of the company but it was one of three in the book but I remember the number I called from the time of the order the date of the order the address where I was going—oh—you have that.

Beat.

St. Andre—2418—the corner of de Bienville... Yes.

Beat.

No—I *called* for it—I already told you that!

LOUISE gestures to her.

(Calm again.) Yes. And I asked for a car with a big trunk...

(She looks at LOUISE.) What? Yes, she's—do you want to talk to her? *(Asking LOUISE.)* Can they call me back on this number?

LOUISE: Of course.

SAMIRA: *(Into the phone.)* You can. Okay. Thank you.

She hangs up.

They need to find the constable who—took care of my case.

LOUISE:	Good.	SAMIRA:	They have everything—his lighter, cigarettes—the crowbar, my… *(She gestures to her clothing.)* And they said because I flagged it—no—sorry—*because I didn't flag it,* it's really good.

LOUISE: *(Beat.)* How are you doing?

SAMIRA: That's what he said—just now. "It's really good you ordered the cab."

Pause.

(Realizing.) He saw me go in.

Beat.

He saw me go in but— *(She looks at LOUISE.)* You can only get in from the lobby.

LOUISE: Get in where?

SAMIRA: The courtyard…he never left! He went straight from the lobby into the courtyard and then… counted out where my back door was on the fire escape—from the one I went into—

LOUISE: From the hallway?

SAMIRA: He was watching—he watched me go down the hallway—that's how he knew which apartment was mine! The boiler room was off the courtyard—they said it was open, remember? It was supposed to be locked but it wasn't because he opened it when he left—*so he could come back later*—that's why they missed him.

Beat.

Write it down—*write it down before I forget!*

Scene Thirteen

Courtyard.

NINA is on the bench, eating a chocolate bar while looking intently at something beside her.

SAMIRA enters, watching her from a distance.

NINA: *(Taking a bite of her bar.)* I know you're there.

SAMIRA comes closer, and spots an emerald ring on the bench.

SAMIRA: Is that yours?

NINA: No. *(Beat.)* It's my mother's.

SAMIRA: It's gorgeous.

NINA: She never does not wear it.

NINA looks at it a moment longer, then picks it up.

(She smiles at SAMIRA.) Okay. There's room now.

SAMIRA sits down. NINA puts the ring back on her finger.

She took it off and put it here so I can feel her with me. *(Showing SAMIRA her hand.)* See?

SAMIRA: That's nice.

NINA: It's not nice—it's amazingly beautiful.

ROSEMARY, forties, stylish, enters. She is carrying a book.

SAMIRA: Hi.

ROSEMARY nods hello, but stays close to the tree.

NINA: *(Hushed, to SAMIRA.)* You should say it now.

SAMIRA: *(To ROSEMARY.)* Did you sign out? They'll chase you out of here/if you don't

NINA: Not that!

SAMIRA: *(To NINA.)* But they will, though…

ROSEMARY: I signed out.

NINA: *(Purposefully, to ROSEMARY.)* "I'm sorry you're here but I'm glad you're here." *(To SAMIRA.)* It was your turn.

Pause.

ROSEMARY: *(Looking up into the tree.)* It's nice here.

NINA: It's my secret place.

ROSEMARY: Not much of a secret.

NINA: Because everyone can see us?

ROSEMARY: Because everyone knows it's here.

NINA: But nobody knows it's my secret place.

SAMIRA: *(Getting up, to ROSEMARY.)* You can sit if you want.

ROSEMARY: Thank you.

ROSEMARY sits down on the bench.

NINA: *(To ROSEMARY.)* Do you have any kids?

ROSEMARY: A boy.

SAMIRA: What's his name?

ROSEMARY: Liam.

NINA: How old is he?

ROSEMARY: Fourteen.

NINA: *(Beat, not unkind.)* So you had him pretty late.

ROSEMARY stares at NINA, who smiles at her, oblivious.

SAMIRA: *(To ROSEMARY.)* Did you get Dr. Lahani or Henderson?

ROSEMARY: Henderson, I think?

NINA: *(To ROSEMARY.)* Did you get varicose veins?

ROSEMARY: Sorry?

NINA: When you were pregnant did you get varicose veins? *(Sticking her legs out in front of her.)* 'Cause I don't have any.

ROSEMARY: Liam is my stepson.

NINA: Your stepson?

ROSEMARY: Yes.

NINA: Oh.

SAMIRA: Okay…gotta go! *(Flashing a smile at ROSEMARY.)* Henderson in five.

NINA: Louise is better though.

SAMIRA: *(To ROSEMARY.)* We all get Louise—

NINA: But you guys only get her "as needed." She's my ONLY doctor.

SAMIRA gives ROSEMARY a look, then goes.

ROSEMARY opens her book and starts to read. NINA takes another bite of her bar.

I'm always hungry… *(Laughs.)* Even when I'm eating!

ROSEMARY smiles.

ROSEMARY: How far along are you?

NINA: Any day now!

ROSEMARY stares — then catching herself — goes back to her book.

(Beat.) How old are you?

ROSEMARY: That's…rude.

NINA: You're probably the same as me! You can have your own baby too if you want to.

ROSEMARY: Liam is my own.

NINA: You know what I mean.

ROSEMARY: *(Looking directly at her.)* No, actually. I don't.

NINA: *(Clarifying — not unkind.)* I mean, he has a *real* mom.

This lands hard on ROSEMARY. She goes back to her book.

(Cupping her breasts.) Owwww! See? We just have to talk about her and bang there she is reminding me…

ROSEMARY: *(Still reading.)* Are they sore?

NINA: *Always.*

ROSEMARY: *(Beat.)* Mine too.

NINA: Really?!

ROSEMARY: All the time. But it's normal—at our age. For what's coming.

NINA: What's coming?!

ROSEMARY: Menopause.

Pause.

(She stands.) I'm going to go find something to eat—want anything?

NINA: No, we're...hey! I got—? *(Offering her chocolate bar.)* You can have half if you want.

ROSEMARY: I need some real food. Thanks, though.

ROSEMARY leaves. NINA eats her chocolate bar for a few beats – stops suddenly – and stares straight ahead.

Scene Fourteen

Cafeteria. Evening.

SAMIRA eats dinner, attention on 'Karen' offstage.

MILDRED and JOYCE place their trays at Samira's table.

JOYCE: *(Looking in the same direction as SAMIRA.)* Karen will sit there all day like that.

MILDRED: Don't look at her! Too much goddamn attention on her as it is. Take it away—see how fast she eats.

JOYCE: The lady with her is a nurse.

SAMIRA: Why does she sit with a nurse?

JOYCE: To make sure she eats everything on her plate. If it was up to Karen she'd eat sunflower seeds all day. They take a long time to get out of the shell so it feels like she's eating more than she is. That's what she told me. She almost died once. So did I. Both times.

MILDRED. For crying out loud!

SAMIRA: I don't…know what / to say.

JOYCE: I'll only know anything about you if you tell me. They have a privacy policy here.

SAMIRA: That's good.

JOYCE: But it's not about protecting our privacy if that's what you're thinking. They don't want us exchanging information.

SAMIRA: What kind of information?

JOYCE: Tips. Or advice. Advice would be worse.

JOYCE catches sight of ROSEMARY in the food line.

Hey, Rosemary! Krista's looking for you/ she has a message

ROSEMARY: I got it.

JOYCE: Is Liam your husband?

ROSEMARY: *(Stops cold.)* You read my message?

JOYCE: No! He wanted Krista to read it back I guess—I was just there.

ROSEMARY: You didn't have to listen.

MILDRED laughs. ROSEMARY moves further down the line.

JOYCE: *(To ROSEMARY.)* You look really familiar.

SAMIRA:	Leave her alone, Joyce.	ROSEMARY:	I don't think so.

JOYCE: I have a gift for faces.

ROSEMARY: *(Beat. To JOYCE.)* I am one hundred percent positive we've never met.

Looking for another place to sit, ROSEMARY exits as LOUISE enters — crossing the room. Seeing her, SAMIRA immediately goes toward her.

JOYCE: Hey—where are you going?!

SAMIRA catches LOUISE.

SAMIRA: Louise!

LOUISE: Oh, hi/ Samira

SAMIRA: The police haven't called back have they?

LOUISE: Not yet.

SAMIRA: I'm making a list of everything I remembered—times, dates, addresses...everything. Will you send it to them? I think it could help.

LOUISE: *(Beat.)* Of course.

Scene Fifteen

Common Room. Evening.

JOYCE makes notes on a "Colour Wheel" at the table. NINA enters with a bottle of nail polish, and sits near JOYCE.

ROSEMARY enters, book in hand. MILDRED, holding a small paper cup, appears in the doorway, and addresses someone offstage.

MILDRED: You know I only ever swallow for you. *(Entering, she chucks her cup.)* That Ivan is one hottie nurse.

NINA: *(Painting her toes.)* I LOVE THIS COLOUR.

JOYCE: That's because you're "warm autumn."

JOYCE is trying hard not to stare at ROSEMARY, who has settled in with her book. NINA looks at the colour wheel.

NINA: And you're "clear spring"!

JOYCE: No—I'm "deep winter." See? *(Beat.)* So are you, Rosemary.

ROSEMARY: *(Reading.)* Hunh.

CELINE enters. SAMIRA follows, mid-conversation.

SAMIRA: She's calling tomorrow—first thing. I'll probably have to go.

MILDRED: Go where?

SAMIRA: Montreal.

CELINE: Would you fly straight from here?

SAMIRA: If they need me right away I'll have to…

SAMIRA sits on the couch. CELINE checks the TV for listings. ROSEMARY goes to the fridge.

ROSEMARY: Why is there never any water in here?!

She slams the fridge door and exits.

JOYCE: *(Beat.)* I've definitely seen her before.

ROSEMARY returns almost immediately. LOUISE follows with a case of bottled water.

LOUISE: Sorry about that, ladies.

JOYCE: *(Intercepting.)* I can do it!

LOUISE: No—that's okay.

JOYCE: *(Taking the case from her.)* But I want to.

LOUISE hands it over and goes. ROSEMARY takes a bottle.

(Stocking the fridge.) You're local, right?

ROSEMARY: More or less.

CELINE: Joyce.

JOYCE: *(To CELINE.)* What's your problem?

CELINE: Privacy maybe?

JOYCE: I never asked her last name!

CELINE: You're still trying to identify her.

JOYCE: Fine. *(Beat. To ROSEMARY.)* What general area/ are you—

CELINE: Omigod!

ROSEMARY: 49449 Cielo Drive, Hillside Estates is where I live.

Pause.

JOYCE: *(To ROSEMARY.)* Do you work at the Hillside Mall?

CELINE: I give up!

MILDRED: She lives in the Estates, why the hell would she work anywhere?!

ROSEMARY: I shop at Hillside Mall.

JOYCE: Well, I go there every two days! I'm a consultant for Mary Kay, so I have to—

MILDRED: Now I know we're in hell.

NINA opens the fridge, and stands there, door wide open. LOUISE enters, memo in hand.

LOUISE: *(To ROSEMARY.)* Liam called again.

ROSEMARY: *(Taking the memo.)* Thanks.

LOUISE: Can you let Liam know to use the number in here? We can't tie up the nurses' station with personal calls.

ROSEMARY: I will. Thanks, Louise.

LOUISE notices NINA at the open fridge.

LOUISE: Something you can't find?

NINA: I'm just hot.

LOUISE goes to her.

LOUISE: Ivan tells me you want to stop the Prozac.

NINA: I did already.

She reaches in her pocket and shows four pills to LOUISE.

LOUISE: This is two days' worth, Nina—you can't just stop like that!

NINA: But I feel better though.

LOUISE: Let's talk in my office.

They leave.

ROSEMARY: I don't blame her.

CELINE: You can't feel better in two days. It takes at least two weeks to get out of your system.

SAMIRA: Prozac makes you aggressive / ...

ROSEMARY: No—it makes men aggressive. Not women.

CELINE: Celexa's better.

MILDRED: If you never want to have sex again maybe!

CELINE: You want to have sex now anyway?

MILDRED: Would I have to go down on you?

They laugh.

CELINE: GOD. I just want to watch a good movie!

SAMIRA: Have you checked the library?

CELINE: Here—? Are you kidding?

MILDRED: Kids and animals.

CELINE: Not even.

MILDRED: Yeah—we'd be on suicide watch for days after *Old Yeller*!

CELINE: *(Laughing, she leaves.)* I'll go check.

Pause.

JOYCE: *(To ROSEMARY.)* Do you have a dog?

MILDRED: CHRIST ROSEMARY SAY YOU HAVE A DOG.

ROSEMARY: Al has her—a little white Shih Tzu –

JOYCE: Popcorn! ROSEMARY: Popcorn—

ROSEMARY: —what?

JOYCE: *(To everyone.)* I TOLD YOU I KNEW YOU! That Richard Dressler workshop in Westwood!

ROSEMARY: *(Shocked.)* You were there?

JOYCE: Well everyone said if you're going to start swinging you gotta go to Richard's Swing School!

MILDRED: Swing school?!

JOYCE: *(Excited.)* Yeah—to learn boundaries and stuff: what I "do," what I "don't do"—full swap, soft swap / safe words

SAMIRA: *(Laughing.)* Omigod!

JOYCE: *(To ROSEMARY.)* Personally, I loved Richard—Bill not so much but he never likes anything that costs anything, so it's a miracle he even went, but your husband…uh…

ROSEMARY: Al.

JOYCE: Al! Right! I was so nervous! *(Addressing the group.)* So to help us relax he made us stand in a circle / and say—

SAMIRA: Who, Al?

JOYCE: *(Flustered.)* No—*Richard*—sorry, I'm just so—okay, Richard, tells us to all hold hands and say, "The Awkward Is Upon Us"—all together three times before we took anything off/ and then—

SAMIRA: *(Cutting her off.)* You got naked with Al?!

MILDRED: Holy shit!

JOYCE: *(Quickly, to ROSEMARY.)* We didn't DO anything though! Richard just asked us questions—like... We each had to say something we liked—like, "I like"—and then something sexual like, "I like blow jobs," or, "I like—my boobs," or...but I just got so nervous when he got to me I said, "I like... DOGS!" And everybody laughed—like you guys now—but Al

(To ROSEMARY.) Your Al jumps in and says, "SO DO I!" And I just liked him right away because Bill, my own husband, was laughing like I was some kind of idiot, not because I was cute.

ROSEMARY: *(Beat.)* And... Popcorn?

JOYCE: After—in the parking lot—Al told me he really did like dogs and had a little white Shih Tzu called Popcorn! *I told you*—I have a gift for faces. And you didn't even stay five minutes.

ROSEMARY: I had a headache.

MILDRED snorts.

When Al was finished...playing...we went home.

JOYCE: "Playing Well with Others: An Introduction to the Art of Swinging." The name of our workshop Rosemary and me took together.

MILDRED: *(Looking at ROSEMARY.)* HOLY…

SAMIRA: SHIT!

SAMIRA and MILDRED dissolve into laughter.

Scene Sixteen

Bedroom. Afternoon.

SAMIRA, on the bed, watches as ROSEMARY folds her personal laundry. They are mid-conversation.

ROSEMARY: I fell in love with him first, you know. Not Al. He was horrible. The first time I stayed over, he told me not to eat his "daddy's cereal."

SAMIRA: How old was he?

ROSEMARY: Three. I was determined to make friends so I asked him for something to play with. He threw me a truck with one wheel and a headless Barbie.

SAMIRA laughs.

I played with them every morning for two weeks straight—but he still wouldn't play with me. One night he got croup. Al carried him for hours—when all of a sudden he leaned towards me—reaching for *me,* not Al. Two minutes later he threw up in my hair.

SAMIRA: *(Laughing.)* What did you do?

ROSEMARY: I didn't let go. Neither did he.

ROSEMARY picks up the book she's been reading and takes out a photo stuck inside. She hands it to SAMIRA.

SAMIRA: He's so cute!

ROSEMARY: Thank you.

SAMIRA: *(Beat.)* I know it's biologically impossible but he looks like you.

ROSEMARY laughs, pleased.

ROSEMARY: It's the expression…

She sits next to SAMIRA, who looks more closely.

SAMIRA: *(Laughs.)* Oh yeah—that's the face *you* make… Maybe that's why people say I look like Mummy when I don't at all!

ROSEMARY: Are you close?

SAMIRA: Yeah. *(Beat.)* She told me once she trusted me with her life but not my own.

ROSEMARY: You'll understand when you have your own children.

SAMIRA hands the photo back to ROSEMARY.

SAMIRA: How come you never had kids?

ROSEMARY: I *do* have a kid—

SAMIRA: That's not what I/ meant—

ROSEMARY: Well I'm getting really sick of hearing it.

She gets up to tuck the photo back inside her book. After a moment SAMIRA gets up to go –

Wait. What's going on with your—?

SAMIRA: We have a Skype call with the police next week.

ROSEMARY: That's good.

SAMIRA: Yeah.

As Samira is leaving –

ROSEMARY: *(Quietly.)* Al didn't want any more. Kids. And once I met Liam… I was working two jobs trying to save for university when he came into my life. After that all I wanted to do was stay at home with him. *(Beat.)* I don't know how to do anything else.

SAMIRA: Other than what?

ROSEMARY: Be a family.

Scene Seventeen

Courtyard. Afternoon.

CELINE leans against the wall, smoking…and waiting. We hear what sounds like a bus, stopping, followed by a sudden explosion of chattering children tumbling out of a school bus — parents honking, the happy calling out of names and of course, some crying. Mayhem.

LOUISE approaches.

CELINE: *(Referring to the sounds outside the gate.)* My happy place.

They listen together as it dissipates.

LOUISE: What did Mohammed say?

CELINE: Stay as long as I want. Whatever I need to do for Adam.

LOUISE: *(Beat.)* I'd like to schedule a couple's session for you and Mohammed.

CELINE: He won't come.

LOUISE: I'd still like to ask him.

Pause.

CELINE: "My lover asks me, what is the difference between me and the sky? The difference, my love, is that when you laugh, I forget about the sky."

LOUISE: Beautiful. What is it?

CELINE: An Arabic poem Mohammed says to me. *(Beat.)* I have a husband who loves me, Louise, but I know what he can handle.

LOUISE: If Mohammed can handle what happened to Adam, he can handle / what happened to you

CELINE: He didn't handle anything—*I* did. He said he couldn't bear to watch Adam show us—what—*(Beat, she takes a drag from her cigarette.)* He showed me on a doll. I crawled around behind him for a whole year staring down that dirty, broken doll. He kicked it—jumped on it—but he never once touched it. Adam had a cold that day… Mohammed drove us—I didn't want to cancel. I don't know if it was his fever or what, but he—picked it up, he—grabbed it up in his tiny little hands—breathing so hard—pulling and pulling… He tore that doll to pieces. And for the first time since it happened… Adam cried.

Beat.

Mohammed missed the whole thing. He was waiting in the car.

LOUISE: *(Beat.)* Keeping what you've been through from him isn't working anymore. You wouldn't be here if it was.

CELINE: I'm not keeping anything from him. He's not asking.

LOUISE: You walked through fire for Adam, Celine. Let Mohammed do the same for you.

CELINE: *(Beat.)* I was high on coke having sex for money when I met Mohammed, Louise. If he can't look at his baby's hell, how is he going to live with mine?

A lingering cry of a child outside, a parent's entreaty…

Mohammed wants to protect Adam from a mother in slippers and a housecoat. Who's going to protect him from a mother who trusts the wrong people?

LOUISE: You were entrusted to the wrong people, Celine.

CELINE: But this time they got my child. And I'm the one who handed him over.

Scene Eighteen

Common Room. Evening.

MILDRED and NINA play Scrabble at the table. SAMIRA plays too.

JOYCE keeps score while watching a show on South Indian temples. ROSEMARY watches with her. They all drink tea from Styrofoam cups.

JOYCE: I'm going there one day. *(Beat, to ROSEMARY.)* Have you?

ROSEMARY: Once. Backpacking.

JOYCE:	I can't imagine you backpacking!	MILDRED:	CELINE!

JOYCE: And China. You can't live in the world and not see the Great Wall of China.

ROSEMARY: That's weird.

MILDRED: *(To SAMIRA.)* Can't you go for her?

JOYCE:	What's weird?	SAMIRA:	No.

ROSEMARY: I was just reading about these performance artists who wanted to get married there.

JOYCE: Really?

CELINE rushes in and resumes her place at the table.

CELINE:	*(Teasing, to everyone.)* Ivan's on…	ROSEMARY:	By the time they got their permits, they weren't in love anymore.

MILDRED snorts.

ROSEMARY: They went anyway, though.

JOYCE: What for?

ROSEMARY: To say goodbye in a meaningful way.

MILDRED: *(To ROSEMARY.)* Give me a break!

ROSEMARY: *(To MILDRED.)* They were together for fourteen years.

JOYCE: They just went there and hugged?

ROSEMARY: No — they walked towards each other from opposite ends of the wall and when / they met in the middle

JOYCE: How long did that take?

ROSEMARY: Three months / —

CELINE:	*(Listening, plays her word.)* This isn't going to end well.	ROSEMARY:	—And when they finally met in the middle… he told her he was having an affair with their Chinese translator and now she was pregnant.

CELINE: Told you. *(Checking her score.)* Eighteen — double word score!

MILDRED: *(To JOYCE.)* Eighteen for Celine, Joyce. Nina go.

JOYCE: That's a terrible story.

ROSEMARY: I don't know. Even if there was another woman, he still walked for three months to tell her that. Al walked in the door, said, "I met someone, she's pregnant, Liam's coming with me," turned around and left. Took him less than a minute.

Pause.

MILDRED: *(To NINA.)* It's not rocket science!

CELINE: *(To NINA.)* Are you even here?

NINA looks at her blankly, then plays her word.

MILDRED: What the hell is that?

NINA: *(Checking her score.)* Four plus one plus two. Triple word score.

<table><tr><td>CELINE:</td><td>Wow.</td><td>JOYCE:</td><td>(At the TV.) That's from one rock? They carved that out of ONE rock!</td></tr></table>

CELINE: Twenty-one for Nina, Joyce.

<table><tr><td>MILDRED:</td><td>She made it up!</td><td>NINA:</td><td>Twenty-one! Write. It. Down.</td></tr></table>

JOYCE: *(Still focused on the TV.)* That is UN-believable!

<table><tr><td>ROSEMARY:</td><td>(Taking the pad from JOYCE.) I'll do it.</td><td>MILDRED:</td><td>(To SAMIRA.) Check it first.</td></tr></table>

SAMIRA checks the dictionary.

NINA: *(Beat.)* It is so a word.

SAMIRA: *(Reading.)* "Vug: Noun. A cavity in a rock formed when rock crystals grow and are then eroded or washed away, leaving a void."

JOYCE: *(To SAMIRA.)* It's a *rock*?

SAMIRA: A void in a rock.

JOYCE: *(Looking at the TV.)* It's like I'm psychic!

NINA: Number six on the "Top Ten Odd Scrabble Words" list.

ROSEMARY: *(Writing.)* Twenty-one for Nina.

NINA: *(Picking more tiles.)* This game is definitely NOT boring!

MILDRED: She's a liar. *(To NINA.)* You're a liar.

NINA: *(Standing.)* We need to go have a little lie-/down now—

MILDRED: THERE IS NO BABY IN THERE NO BABY YOU ARE AS FLAT *(Grabbing the board off the table.)* AS THIS BOARD YOU CAN BEND DOWN LIE FLAT ON YOUR STOMACH BECAUSE YOU ARE SAD YOU ARE SAD DO YOU HEAR ME? BE FUCKING SAD.

The women sit stunned. NINA unconsciously places her hand on her stomach.

NINA: I don't—I…

Then, carefully stepping over the spilt tiles, she leaves.

Beat.

ROSEMARY: *(To MILDRED.)* You're a bully.

She follows NINA out.

CELINE heads into the kitchen. JOYCE packs up the game. No one speaks.

MILDRED: I'm not playing her crazy game anymore/—you all can!

SAMIRA: It's not a game.

JOYCE: *(To MILDRED.)* Do you know where she was today?

MILDRED: Shock therapy, I hope.

JOYCE: She had a sonogram this afternoon!

MILDRED: GOOD.

JOYCE stares at MILDRED, then leaves.

CELINE: *(To MILDRED.)* What's wrong with you? You're not stupid so what the hell is it? Tell me.

MILDRED turns her back. Reluctantly, CELINE leaves.

MILDRED: *(Out the door.)* Hey, Ivan! I'll blow you for a Tylenol.

Still at the table, SAMIRA quietly observes MILDRED.

Scene Nineteen

Courtyard. Early morning.

SAMIRA, on the bench and wrapped in a blanket, writes in her journal. CELINE, in slippers and a bathrobe, with a mug of hot tea in hand, enters.

CELINE: *(Beat. Teasing.)* So this is what you're up to when the animals are asleep.

SAMIRA: *(Preoccupied.)* Huh?

Looking up, she sees CELINE.

Oh, sorry—I was just… What are you doing up?

CELINE: I never went to sleep. *(Beat.)* You're actually writing something in there?

SAMIRA: I actually felt like it.

CELINE: And I interrupted you.

SAMIRA: No… *(Lifting the blanket.)* Sit with me.

Sitting at opposite ends of the bench, CELINE and SAMIRA share the blanket between them.

(Closing her journal.) I wasn't really in the mood anyway.

CELINE: What mood do you have to be in?

SAMIRA: Suicidal.

They laugh.

CELINE: Read me some.

SAMIRA: Are you crazy?!

CELINE: I had a terrible night.

SAMIRA: You're such a con-ner…!

She opens the journal to its first page.

Fine. But it's stupid. *(Reading.)* "It never goes away. Every happiness will be measured against the weight of its presence or the surprise of its absence. It is beyond telling, and beyond listening…" *(Hiding her face.)* IT'S TOO CORNY!

CELINE laughs.

See—you're laughing!

CELINE: I'm laughing at you, dummy. Go on.

SAMIRA: *(Beat.)* "But there is Beauty in me too. I can't see it now, but they do. The people I love—who will not let me go."

SAMIRA, embarrassed, laughs again. CELINE doesn't.

"Because they will not, I will stay. Then one day, I will stay because I see what they see, and I will know I am more than this and death will no longer be part of every day of my life. I will know—"

SAMIRA stops short, unable to continue.

CELINE: *(Beat.)* Can I?

SAMIRA shrugs. CELINE takes the journal from her.

(Reading.) "I will know…that even though it never goes away, I will learn to bear it. I will fight for them; I will fight for me…"

Reading ahead, CELINE stops, hit hard by something she's read.

"I will fight for what can be, still… Love will be my weapon."

SAMIRA looks down at a page full of words that, for the first time in years, she might be able to live by.

Scene Twenty

Common Room. Evening.

MILDRED stares blankly at the TV, remote in hand.

ROSEMARY reads her book at the table, sipping tea.

There is no sound but the TV; the air is still somewhat charged from the last time everyone was together in this room.

JOYCE enters with a glass bowl of ice cream. It takes her some time to decide where to sit — far enough away from Mildred, but still able to see the TV.

She begins to mix her ice cream; the spoon scraping the sides of the bowl…

MILDRED: *(Eyes fixed on the TV.)* What are you doing?

JOYCE: Nothing. Mixing.

Pause.

MILDRED: What?

JOYCE: Ice cream.

JOYCE continues mixing for a few beats.

MILDRED: Quit it.

ROSEMARY: It is kind of annoying, Joyce.

JOYCE: Oh. Sorry. I always have to make it into a pudding first.

JOYCE tries to mix more quietly. MILDRED stares.

I can't eat it if there's lumps!

MILDRED turns back to the TV.

JOYCE begins to eat her ice cream: dipping her spoon in, flipping it over, then licking the ice cream from it; in the process, ROSEMARY suddenly twigs to the sound of the spoon against the bowl.

ROSEMARY: *(To JOYCE.)* Hey—how'd you get away with that?!

JOYCE: I wasn't finished so she said do you want to take it to go so I said yes.

ROSEMARY: In a *glass* bowl?!

JOYCE: *(Shrugging it off.)* Yeah.

ROSEMARY: You better not get caught with it down here…

At some point during the following exchange, MILDRED clocks Joyce's "flip/lick" ritual and focuses in on it.

They're not kidding, Joyce!

JOYCE: *Okay*. Stop talking now.

Pause.

MILDRED: *(Quietly, to JOYCE.)* What are you doing?

JOYCE: Why does it bug you so much?

She continues eating, ignoring MILDRED.

MILDRED: *(Not taking her eyes off JOYCE.)* Quit it.

JOYCE: Quit what?

ROSEMARY: *(To MILDRED.)* Ignore her.

MILDRED: QUIT IT.

JOYCE: No.

MILDRED: Quit *doing*/ that…

JOYCE: *(Looking at the TV.)* Not quitting…

ROSEMARY: *(Gathering her things.)* This is ridiculous.

MILDRED: QUIT IT I SAID.

JOYCE: *(Digging her spoon in.)* YOU. *(Flipping it over.)* FUCK. *(She licks.)* OFF.

MILDRED suddenly whacks the bowl from JOYCE's hands.

HEY!

ROSEMARY: OH MY GOD!

MILDRED lunges for the flying bowl, missing it. It breaks. She gasps. JOYCE and ROSEMARY, stunned, watch as MILDRED gathers the broken pieces and cradles them. She begins to breathe heavily, fighting against it; she "consoles" the bowl as if it were a small bird.

(Quietly.) Mildred?

MILDRED is making a superhuman effort to push back the oncoming grief.

(To JOYCE.) Get someone.

MILDRED loses the battle: a cry of animal anguish unleashed from deep inside. JOYCE can't move —

GET SOMEONE!

JOYCE goes. ROSEMARY crawls to MILDRED; landing near but not touching.

SAMIRA, appearing in the doorway, has her eyes fixed squarely on MILDRED.

Clutching the broken pieces to her, MILDRED finally weeps.

Act II

Scene One

Common Room. Later.

LOUISE, dressed for a night out, searches for something in the kitchen area. NINA, in a flannel nightie, watches LOUISE from a distance.

NINA: You look nice.

LOUISE: I was on my way out.

NINA: For a date?

LOUISE doesn't respond. NINA tries again, louder this time.

Are you going on a date?

LOUISE: No.

NINA: You look like you're going on a date.

NINA goes to the fridge and takes out a yogurt.

What are you looking for?

LOUISE: Something broke.

NINA: *(Surprised.)* Broke?

LOUISE: Joyce took a glass bowl out of the cafeteria.

NINA: Oh boy.

LOUISE: The girl was a temp. She didn't know.

NINA gets down on her hands and knees to help look.

Nina. I got it.

NINA: *(Still looking.)* We'll find it. Only later. Like, I'll find that ring my mom gave me—only later.

LOUISE: You lost your ring?

NINA: I turned it around and around on my finger like I always do before I go to sleep, but when I woke up this morning it was gone.

LOUISE: Oh, Nina!

NINA: Nobody took it off my finger when I was sleeping because I sleep on my hands, so it has to be in my room somewhere.

LOUISE: I'll help you look after / I'm finished here

NINA: I don't want to look. If I look and can't find it, that means it's really gone. If I don't look, it means it's still there. I just can't find it right *now.*

LOUISE picks up three broken pieces and fits them together.

Maybe there is no other piece. Maybe we're looking for something that isn't even there. *(Beat.)* I'm not saying that because I have it.

Pause.

I'm going to think it isn't there. We're not going to find it later this time because it isn't there.

She goes.

LOUISE looks at the broken bowl, then gets down on her hands and knees, trying to see beneath the fridge: first her hand — then arm — reaching under. Her body — now face — flatten against the floor, reaching further still.

Scene Two

Common Room. Afternoon.

NINA, CELINE, ROSEMARY, JOYCE, SAMIRA and LOUISE sit in a circle on the floor. A woven red cloth lies in the middle.

CELINE turns an elaborately carved "Talking Stick" over and over in her hands. JOYCE tentatively raises her hand.

LOUISE: Celine has the stick, Joyce.

CELINE: Sorry.

LOUISE: You can just hold it if you like. You don't have to say anything if you don't want to.

NINA: I didn't know that!

Hesitating, CELINE finally speaks.

CELINE: I wanted Michael to be our babysitter. Mohammed didn't want to leave Adam with anyone, but Michael was our best friends' son. When I started to show, he would talk to my belly. *(Beat.)* Is that…weird? Letting a teenaged boy talk to your belly? I thought it was sweet.

CELINE puts the stick down on the cloth. NINA picks it up, holds it for a few moments, then puts it down again. CELINE and ROSEMARY reach for it at the same time.

CELINE: Oh—sorry! ROSEMARY: No, you go ahead—

CELINE: *(Taking it.)* I just wanted to say I'm also really worried about Mildred.

CELINE hands it to ROSEMARY, then remembers to put it back on the cloth. ROSEMARY picks it up.

ROSEMARY: We're all friends now, so I'd like to address something that was said—a while ago—that was really upsetting/ to me

JOYCE: By somebody here?!

ROSEMARY realizes her mistake.

LOUISE: Go ahead, Rosemary.

ROSEMARY: Before—everything—Liam and I were spending the day together... We like to walk—and we saw some shawls in a window. There was a blue one—Liam immediately picked it up and said, "Do you think Mum would like this?" For a flash I thought—"I'm right here"—it was just a flash, not even a second—of course I knew he was talking about his mother. I didn't feel bad, though. I felt proud. He asked me that question because he felt safe enough to ask it. And loved. *(Beat.)* I think that makes me as real a mom as anyone.

She puts the Stick back down. The women try not to look like they're trying to guess to whom this was directed.

LOUISE: Anyone else? Okay. Once again I'd like to thank Elder Mae Margaret for the teachings and the blessing to use the Talking Stick in our work today. Miigwetch. Thank you. *(Beat.)* In this same spirit, I want to say we still haven't found that missing piece of glass. I'm not accusing /anyone

NINA: How do you know there even is a piece though?

LOUISE: I don't. It could be in the garbage—or swept up...but for your own safety, room checks are taking place/ respectfully

CELINE: What?! JOYCE: Right now?

CELINE immediately gets up and leaves.

ROSEMARY: You can't search someone's room without their permission "respectfully."

LOUISE: You're welcome to be present if you like.

ROSEMARY: Or you could've just asked but you /didn't because you are accusing us!

NINA: My ring.

JOYCE: You lost your ring?

NINA: *(Panicking.) What if they don't find my ring, Louise?!*

LOUISE: Nina.

NINA: *(Completely unravelling.)* THEY'RE GOING TO LOOK FOR THAT GLASS EVERY SINGLE PLACE IN MY ROOM AND IF THEY DON'T FIND THE GLASS AND THEY DON'T FIND MY RING—

LOUISE goes to her.

NINA: *(Escalating.)* IT MEANS IT'S REALLY, REALLY/ GONE—

LOUISE: We'll stop them/come on…

LOUISE removes NINA from the room.

Pause.

SAMIRA: Well if she is hiding it that was fucking brilliant.

ROSEMARY goes to make tea. SAMIRA stretches out her lower back on the floor. JOYCE stays where she is.

I don't know why everyone's so worried about Mildred.

JOYCE: She had a breakdown!

SAMIRA: *(Sharply.)* No, she didn't! *(Beat.)* She remembered something.

JOYCE: Too bad she had to attack me first to do it.

ROSEMARY: She did not *attack* you, Joyce.

JOYCE: She came at me like a crazy person—you were there!

ROSEMARY: She wasn't attacking you! You obviously triggered something /for her

JOYCE: What if she triggered me? WHAT ABOUT THAT?

ROSEMARY: Well you're in here and she's in her room so / obviously she didn't.

SAMIRA: *(To JOYCE.)* Are you okay?

JOYCE: I am *now.*

Pause.

When did—*(She stops.)*

SAMIRA: What?

JOYCE: Yours… /happen.

SAMIRA: Five years ago.

JOYCE: Where did/ it—

ROSEMARY: Joyce.

SAMIRA: *(Beat.)* My apartment.

JOYCE: Was it a date?

SAMIRA: No.

JOYCE: Did they ever catch/ the…?

ROSEMARY: Joyce. SAMIRA: No.

JOYCE: Because you /couldn't

ROSEMARY slams the kettle down.

SAMIRA: Because even though he bashed in my door at two in the morning not one person in my building called 911.

JOYCE: Oh.

SAMIRA: They had hours to do it but no one bothered so he got away.

JOYCE: *(Beat.)* I didn't—I mean I knew—I just didn't know it was... /like that.

SAMIRA: I feel like I'm watching me talk to you right now.

JOYCE: What?

SAMIRA: Rapetorturedinnerabath. Like reading the phone book.

CELINE storms in.

(To CELINE.) How was it?

CELINE: Fucking violating.

Overwhelmed with her own powerlessness, she throws herself on the couch; the other women recognize this.

ROSEMARY: Can I make you some tea?

CELINE: I am not putting up with this shit anymore! *(Beat.)* Mildred's leaving too if anyone cares.

SAMIRA: *(Surprised.)* She is?

ROSEMARY: How do you know?

CELINE: Because they're calling her daughter/ right now

ROSEMARY: That doesn't /mean—

CELINE: *To come pick her up.*

JOYCE: When?

CELINE: Tomorrow afternoon.

SAMIRA gets up quickly.

She's not there. They took her for some meeting.

SAMIRA: When are we supposed to see her then?

CELINE: I don't know.

ROSEMARY: *(To SAMIRA.)* Let's get dinner. She'll be back by the time we're done.

SAMIRA: *(Beat, to CELINE.)* Are you coming…?

CELINE: Just go. I'm fine.

SAMIRA and ROSEMARY leave.

JOYCE: *(Looking at the Talking Stick.)* Someone should probably…

JOYCE wraps it in its cloth through the following:

Did you know about Samira?

CELINE: Yes.

JOYCE: Everything?

CELINE: Everything she wanted to tell me, Joyce.

JOYCE: She said torture.

CELINE: So.

JOYCE: What does that mean?

CELINE: I don't know.

JOYCE: *(Quietly.)* Maybe I do.

CELINE: No. You don't.

JOYCE: How do you know that I don't?

CELINE: *(Getting up.)* I can't do this today.

JOYCE: I'm talking, Celine!

CELINE: I'm not doing this with you today, Joyce—

JOYCE: *(Getting up too.)* But I'm talking!

CELINE makes her way out.

How do you know that I don't, Celine?

JOYCE, alone, the Talking Stick gripped in her hands.

HOW DO YOU KNOW THAT I DON'T, CELINE?

Scene Three

LOUISE's office. Morning.

LOUISE and SAMIRA — for the first time wearing a dress — sit at the table, a speaker phone in front of them. The CONSTABLE on the phone speaks with a French-Canadian accent.

SAMIRA: *(Lightly.)* When you didn't call back I / thought...

CONSTABLE: Yes, I'm so sorry about that, Samira. These things can take time.

SAMIRA: That's okay.

CONSTABLE: Dr. Stratton? Are you there?

LOUISE: Yes, I'm here. SAMIRA: She's here.

SAMIRA: Did you get the list? I sent it / after we spoke

CONSTABLE: Yes, thank you! It was very detailed — very helpful.

SAMIRA: I wrote some times down, too. I remembered them later.

CONSTABLE: *(Beat.)* Before we go on, I want you to know how much I...admire you — for doing this today. *(Beat.)* We have a LOT of good evidence — fingerprints, a rare blood type — if we had a suspect we could identify him very easily.

SAMIRA: We do have a suspect. The taxi driver.

CONSTABLE: Yes. *(Beat.)* There seems to be a statute of limitations on the records kept by taxi companies in the province of Quebec and...until very recently, every few years, they...delete them.

SAMIRA: Delete?

CONSTABLE: The records. *(Beat.)* The records. The...taxi company records.

Pause.

SAMIRA: When?

CONSTABLE: *(With difficulty.)* They deleted them...four years ago.

SAMIRA sits stunned, unable to move.

Scene Four

Bedroom. Later.

LOUISE enters.

LOUISE: Mildred? Are you here?

MILDRED emerges from her bathroom holding two shampoo bottles.

MILDRED: Hardly used these. Guess you can tell!

LOUISE: You know I'm advising against this.

MILDRED: That's why I'm checking myself out.

MILDRED continues packing.

Checked myself in, so I can check myself out.

LOUISE: Dr. Henderson would like to talk to you /again before you go.

MILDRED: You're all so in love with talking: YAP YAP YAP YAP YAP! Shut up for a second and see what happens.

LOUISE: *(Beat.)* We can't force you to stay.

She leaves. MILDRED sits down heavily on the bed.

SAMIRA appears at the door.

SAMIRA: I couldn't find you last night.

MILDRED: *(Immediately getting up.)* They had a lot to say last night.

MILDRED disappears into the bathroom. JOYCE arrives.

JOYCE: *(To SAMIRA.)* She here?

MILDRED emerges with a bag and dumps it in the suitcase.

You're really going?

MILDRED: *(Struggling to close her suitcase.)* If I ever get this crap thing closed I am!

JOYCE: I'll sit on it.

JOYCE sits on it, but they still can't get it closed.

MILDRED: *(Laughing.)* WHAT IN HELL IS IN HERE?

JOYCE: *(Laughing, pointing at MILDRED's outfit.)* And you only ever wore that!

Somehow they manage to zip it up. They stand there together, awkward again.

I know we're not friends or anything, but I want you to be happy.

MILDRED: You too, Joyce.

JOYCE: Okay. Bye.

JOYCE leaves. SAMIRA hasn't moved from the door.

SAMIRA: What you remembered.

MILDRED: Yeah.

SAMIRA: Did it—come all at once or—in pieces/ or…

MILDRED: It just came.

SAMIRA: In a picture?

MILDRED: A feeling.

SAMIRA: What kind of feeling?

MILDRED: Like when that doctor ripped me open. *(Beat.)* Like that.

Pause.

SAMIRA: What happens now?

MILDRED: Chicken and waffles with my girl!

SAMIRA: Have you told her yet?

MILDRED: No.

SAMIRA: When are you going to?

MILDRED: I was six. We never saw him again.

SAMIRA: *(Beat.)* You knew him?

MILDRED: Yeah. An uncle. *(Beat.)* Now listen—I don't do that e-mail shit. I'm going to give/ you my number.

SAMIRA: She's going to find out.

MILDRED: *(Looking for something to write on.)* Not if I don't tell her she won't.

SAMIRA: At court she will.

MILDRED: I'm not going to court.

SAMIRA: You're letting him get away with it?

MILDRED: Yeah—I'm letting some old fuck in diapers now get away /with it —

SAMIRA: But you know who it is!

MILDRED: —I want to be done with it.

SAMIRA: NO—no—he needs to go/ to jail—

MILDRED: I'm done with it.

SAMIRA: He needs to /go to jail!

MILDRED: WHY? WHY DOES HE NEED TO GO TO JAIL?!

SAMIRA: THEY'LL RAPE HIM THERE.

MILDRED: Then what? Then what?

SAMIRA: He knows what it feels like.

Pause.

MILDRED: He'll never know that.

SAMIRA: Because you won't press charges!

MILDRED: I want my kids. Not chasing after what I can't change.

SAMIRA: WON'T/change—

MILDRED: I'm tired.

SAMIRA: You're a coward.

MILDRED: Very, very tired.

SAMIRA: *(Barely holding it together.)* YOU'RE A COWARD.

MILDRED takes a long look at SAMIRA. Then with both hands, she tenderly holds her face. SAMIRA lets her.

Scene Five

Common Room. Early morning.

ROSEMARY sits alone at the long table. The phone is ringing. She doesn't move. It stops.

After a few moments, it starts to ring again — and again, longer than it should. It stops as LOUISE sticks her head in. She is surprised to see ROSEMARY at the table.

LOUISE: Oh—you're here. Liam called.

ROSEMARY: Yes.

LOUISE: I told him to call through here.

ROSEMARY: Okay.

LOUISE: *(Beat.)* Is he coming to Family Day tomorrow?

ROSEMARY: I don't know. I didn't speak to him.

LOUISE: Everything okay, Rosemary?

ROSEMARY: Everything's fine, Louise.

LOUISE steps out into the hallway again.

Are you going to write that down?

LOUISE: *(Stepping back into the room.)* Write what down?

ROSEMARY: That I said everything was fine after missing Liam's call so obviously I don't care about him. Make sure you tell Al.

LOUISE: Asking you to seek treatment before any discussion of Liam's future is not an unreasonable request. *(Beat.)* You almost died, Rosemary.

ROSEMARY: And I get punished for that forever?

LOUISE: It's not a punishment. But we can start looking at next / steps now.

ROSEMARY: When he was little we were at the mercy of his mother. Now I'm at the mercy of his father. Even a mother who beats her kids or a father who rapes his daughters has more rights as a biological parent than I do right now.

LOUISE: We're doing this because you do have rights.

ROSEMARY: That's not really true though, is it? I don't have any legal rights—not without being married to Al. What I should have is enormous gratitude for the privilege of being judged by you at all.

She brushes past LOUISE like a tornado, leaving her slightly stunned.

Scene Six

Courtyard. Night.

ROSEMARY stands on one side of the tree, JOYCE is on the other. CELINE stands against the gate, smoking.

ROSEMARY: She leaves a hole, doesn't she?

CELINE: Mildred? Oh yeah.

JOYCE: Only because she took up so much space.

ROSEMARY moves to the bench.

ROSEMARY: Did Samira come down to eat today?

CELINE: No.

ROSEMARY: She didn't eat yesterday either.

JOYCE: They'll move her upstairs if she keeps this up. That's what they did to Karen.

ROSEMARY: How long before they do that?

JOYCE: Krista said three days.

ROSEMARY: *(Worried.)* Tomorrow's three for Samira.

JOYCE: If you're a danger to yourself, game over.

CELINE: We're already a danger to ourselves.

JOYCE: We're not actively pursuing it/ though

CELINE: Unless you're the one hiding that piece of glass.

JOYCE: Don't joke about that stuff, Celine.

Pause.

CELINE: I'm not worried about Samira.

JOYCE: Really? I thought you guys were "best / friends..."

CELINE: She read me some of her writing.

ROSEMARY: *(Surprised.)* She did?

CELINE: *(Trying to quote.)* I'll fight—for what still can be... something like that.

JOYCE: If she believed that, she wouldn't be starving herself right now.

CELINE: I didn't say she believed it—I said she wrote it. But you don't think about something being possible...unless you can see the days ahead. *(Beat. To ROSEMARY.)* I told Mohammed they want us to do a couple's session.

ROSEMARY: You're kidding.

CELINE: *(Incredulous.)* No.

ROSEMARY: Does that mean you're going to...tell /him about...?

CELINE: I don't know. But I think I want to.

Pause.

JOYCE: Is Adam ever coming to visit?

CELINE: No.

JOYCE: Why not?

CELINE: He's only four. He won't understand he's only visiting.

JOYCE: Really? *(Beat.)* Where does he think you went?

CELINE: Why do you care so much?

JOYCE: I just think it's harder for a four-year-old to understand not seeing you at all than seeing you here.

This hits CELINE hard.

CELINE: (*To ROSEMARY.*) I'm going up. I want to see Samira.

JOYCE: Did anyone notice she stopped eating right after Mildred took off? People think they can just do and say whatever they want around here like it's nothing. It has an effect.

CELINE: *(Laughs.)* On you, you mean.

JOYCE: Yes, on me. Yes, on me…

CELINE leaves.

You think you're the only one who gets to feel anything around here just because you got raped twice—*(She stops.)*

ROSEMARY: Oh no.

CELINE comes right back.

CELINE: Wow. *(To ROSEMARY.)* She's right, you know. No matter what happened to any one of us, none of it comes close to what she feels. *(To JOYCE.)* You win.

Scene Seven

Hallway. Morning.

NINA sits on the floor outside SAMIRA's bedroom door.

LOUISE stands over her.

LOUISE: Why don't we go to your room?

NINA: I like to be near Samira.

LOUISE: We need privacy, Nina.

NINA: She's not listening.

With some difficulty, in her skirt and heels, LOUISE sits down next to her.

LOUISE: We need you to go back on the antidepressants.

NINA: Why?

LOUISE: They'll help to increase the serotonin levels in your brain. When that happens, you'll feel better.

NINA: But it won't be a real feeling better.

LOUISE: They won't take your emotions away. They'll teach your nerves to transmit chemicals at a non-depressed person's rate. Like training wheels on a bicycle. So you'll be able to cope with your very real emotions.

NINA: *(Beat.)* I'm depressed because my serotonin is low, or my serotonin is low because I'm depressed?

LOUISE: *(Slightly taken aback.)* We don't know.

NINA: Can't they measure it?

LOUISE: The serotonin?

NINA: Yeah.

LOUISE: Not in a living brain.

LOUISE brings out a photo of NINA's sonogram and lays it in front of her. NINA doesn't look.

NINA: What if it's a lie, what you know? *(She lays a hand on her stomach.)* What if this is really real? Just because you don't know a thing doesn't mean it's wrong.

LOUISE: That sonogram isn't wrong.

NINA: How do you know that's true if you're wrong?

LOUISE: Because it's a fact, not an opinion.

NINA: Those pregnancy tests are facts, not opinions, too then.

LOUISE: Your depression triggered your pituitary gland to secrete elevated hormones that mimicked the hormone changes of a real pregnancy. That's why the tests came back positive. They were false positives. Do you understand what I'm telling you?

NINA: My mind made my body believe it's pregnant.

LOUISE: Yes.

NINA: What if my body knows something my mind doesn't know yet? My mind doesn't always know everything. It decides things that are wrong all the time. Maybe my body has a secret.

Pause.

LOUISE: Can you look at this picture, Nina?

NINA: Why?

LOUISE: I want you to tell me what you see.

NINA starts to cry.

NINA: No. You want me to tell you what I don't see.

LOUISE: What don't you see?

NINA: Her face. *(Beat.)* Her amazingly beautiful face so happy to see me.

Scene Eight

Bedroom. Evening.

SAMIRA, wearing the same dress as in Scene Three, sits on the edge of her bed, very still.

LOUISE steps into the room.

SAMIRA: Nothing's coming. They stopped.

LOUISE: *(Beat.)* It took three thousand miles and five years later for you to feel safe enough to remember who it was. But you did remember.

SAMIRA: Not his face. *(Beat.)* Mildred caught it. She—*caught* it she…caught it but she…

LOUISE: Let it go.

Pause.

SAMIRA: I thought…if I lie very, very flat he won't see me… he'll see an empty unmade bed because I was so thin and small and… *(Beat.)* He ordered me to hold the position. I didn't understand what position he wanted me to hold. He was yelling at me and laughing at me because I looked so *stupid*…and then he jerked one leg straight up high, and the other one bent at the knee. "I'm going now. I'm going. Don't look. Don't move. Or I'll fucking kill you." If I don't move…if I don't—move—he will be gone and it will be okay. *(Beat.)* I heard the bedroom door slam. I heard him walk away. I didn't move. My legs were shaking on the inside because I couldn't let them shake on the outside or it wouldn't be okay. I thought, I am still, I am Superman I *can* do it I will do it right and it will be okay. (*Beat.*) A long time I stayed like that. Not moving. Not even breathing. *(Beat. Quietly.)* Then I heard him. *You fucking moved. (Beat.)* He never left. He just pretended. Slammed the door from the inside—walked on the spot. Just stood there quietly, watching me... Watching. I did NOT move. He knows it. I know it. We both know I did it right I did it right what he said. But it's not okay. I did it right and it's not okay. He punished me for doing it right.

Pause.

LOUISE steps further into the room; needing SAMIRA to hear and understand what she's about to say.

LOUISE: When you heard the door smash and those boots running towards you in your bed...your fear wasn't the fear of a woman—it was the terror of a *child*. You pulled the covers over your head—what's the first game a baby believes? Peek-a-boo...a terror so big, if I can't see you, you can't see me.

Pause.

SAMIRA: I didn't look.

LOUISE: He said he was going to kill you.

SAMIRA: *(Beat.)* I never looked.

LOUISE doesn't – can't – respond to this unforgiving girl.

Scene Nine

Common Room. Evening.

CELINE is on the phone.

CELINE: Did Adam go down okay? He hates naps, poor thing. *(Beat.)* Has he asked about me at all? *(Beat.)* You don't think that's strange? *(Beat.)* I don't think he is fine, Mohammed…

JOYCE enters. Seeing CELINE, she moves to the kitchen to give her space.

I think he's angry and confused and he doesn't know how to articulate it… I mean, where does he think I went? *(Beat.)* And I think he needs to visit me here. *(Beat.)* You will? No—tomorrow's fine! I'm sure Louise can find someone to watch him while we're with her… We could do a picnic in the courtyard after our session—Adam will love that! *(Beat.)* I don't want to get into that right now. *(Beat.)* Because it's…complicated. And I think Louise should be there. *(Beat.)* Because it's complicated, Mohammed—why do you need to know what we're going to talk about—we're talking about it tomorrow. *(Beat.)* Because I don't think it IS just a simple question, actually!

Silence between them.

Why would you say it's just a simple question? How do you know that?

(Beat.) Because it's not 'simple,' Mohammed, not everything is fucking SIMPLE—

Silence again.

I knew this was going to happen. You want us to fight so now you don't have to come…it's so brilliant. *(Beat.)* I have to go, there's a lineup. *(Beat.)* Go ahead—I won't be there. *(Beat.)* See her on your own then…no—YOU DID THIS.

CELINE slams the phone down hard, but can't let go of it.

JOYCE says nothing.

ROSEMARY bursts in; LOUISE close behind.

ROSEMARY: Handle it, Louise!

LOUISE: I will handle it/ Rosemary but you

ROSEMARY: How did he get here?!

LOUISE: Three buses.

ROSEMARY: Does Al know?!

LOUISE: He must know by now. He said it took him two hours/ to get here

ROSEMARY: Tell him to pick him up—send a car/ I don't care

LOUISE: You can't leave him sitting alone /down there, Rosemary

JOYCE: Liam's here?

ROSEMARY: Call his dad. PLEASE.

LOUISE leaves.

You know what—let him sit there—I didn't tell him to come.

JOYCE: Where is he?

ROSEMARY: In the lobby right now…oh god, what am I going to do?!

CELINE: Go downstairs.

JOYCE:	Celine/…	ROSEMARY:	You have no idea what I'm dealing with/Celine

CELINE: *(To ROSEMARY.)* What is that exactly?

ROSEMARY: *(To JOYCE.)* I'm not doing this with/ her right now—

CELINE: What are you "dealing with?" A boy who loves you who won't take no for an answer/ that's your big problem?

ROSEMARY: You don't know what you're talking about so just/ stop talking—

CELINE: *(Continuing.)* But you don't even say no—you just don't take his calls!

ROSEMARY: *It's complicated*/—

CELINE: *(Dismissive.)* It's not complicated—BE HIS MOTHER.

ROSEMARY: *I'M NOT HIS MOTHER HE HAS A MOTHER I'M NOT HIS FUCKING MOTHER OKAY?!* How many mothers does he need, Celine? What's he going to do—jump from one house to another—his dad's, his mom's—mine now, too?! Every second Saturday—the whole weekend if I'm *good?!* Or maybe he won't even want to come! Maybe he *likes* it there with them and he doesn't want to/ hurt me—*(She stops.)*

LOUISE enters.

Pause.

(Barely keeping it together.) Does anyone ever call you a hero for loving your son? "It's so great how you love Adam…" He's my son. I want to LIVE with my SON. I'd rather be a parent he hates than nobody to him one day.

LOUISE: *(Beat.)* Liam's refusing a cab. He wants to wait the hour for Al to get here.

ROSEMARY stands, then walks out.

JOYCE: *(To LOUISE.)* Is she going?

LOUISE: I don't know.

JOYCE: He's only waiting because of her!

LOUISE: I know.

JOYCE: She just has to see him, Louise/ if she sees him—

LOUISE: I treated a little girl. She was five. She was told never to play alone in the playground after school—to always wait inside. When they found her—three days later—she was naked, raped and left for dead in an abandoned refrigerator. We had been working together a year when one day she said—she was drawing, she loved to draw—she looked up at me and said, Doctor? I'm a good girl. He's a bad man. But I'm a GOOD girl. She knew she'd gone outside alone, talked to a stranger, got into his car—done everything she'd been told not to do.

LOUISE turns to look at JOYCE and CELINE.

If any one of you had even a fraction of the compassion for yourselves that this tiny little girl had for herself—

She stops, unable to continue.

I can't make her go.

LOUISE leaves. JOYCE stares after her. CELINE remains at the phone, very, very still.

Scene Ten

SAMIRA, still in her dress, is on her bed. CELINE appears in the doorway. SAMIRA doesn't acknowledge her.

CELINE walks to the window, and looks out.

SAMIRA: You're leaving.

CELINE: Yes.

SAMIRA: You can't.

CELINE: I need to be with my baby. (*Beat.*) I wanted to say goodbye.

Pause.

SAMIRA: You're never going to tell Mohammed, are you?

CELINE: I don't want to fight, Samira.

SAMIRA: You want him to think Adam is the only reason you're here.

Pause.

CELINE: Under the blanket...that morning when you read me your diary. You said something about beauty... *But there is beauty in me too.*

Beat.

I know you don't see it now. You wouldn't be doing this to yourself if you did.

Beat.

Maybe you'll never see it. Or you'll only see it in the way people love you. But I hope not. I hope, one day, you'll see that beauty all on your own.

CELINE turns to go.

SAMIRA: Can I call you?

Ignoring SAMIRA, she keeps moving.

I want to call you, Celine—

Before CELINE can get out the door –

But I love you.

CELINE freezes.

(Fighting back tears.) Why won't you let me?

Unable to face this girl she loves –

CELINE: I don't want you to know if I don't make it.

CELINE remains in the doorway. SAMIRA, on the bed.

Scene Eleven

Hallway. Night.

JOYCE, unable to sleep in the storm, is headed towards the Common Room. She sees LOUISE.

JOYCE: I was just going to make some tea. Want some?

LOUISE: Can't sleep?

JOYCE: Nope—and apparently I'm not the only one!

They continue into the Common Room, JOYCE leading the way.

He says he can't sleep without me anymore. I told him, "Bill, it doesn't work like that, honey; I can't just—come home." But no… "Enough is enough, Joycey!"

LOUISE pulls a set of keys from her pocket. Seeing them, JOYCE immediately plugs in the kettle, her back to LOUISE.

LOUISE: Bill dropped these off just now…said he'd be gone over a month this time. He thought you might want to ask someone else to water your plants.

LOUISE lays the keys on the counter in front of JOYCE.

I didn't say this to embarrass you, Joyce.

JOYCE: *(Sharply.)* Why'd you say it then?

LOUISE: How long have you been separated?

JOYCE: We're not separated. We're divorced.

LOUISE: How long have you been divorced?

JOYCE: Two years.

LOUISE: *(Beat.)* You don't think that's something Dr. Henderson should have known?

JOYCE: I'm not depressed because Bill left. He left because I was depressed. I'm not here because of Bill.

Opening the cupboard, she picks out a box of tea.

(Beat.) I tried to keep it to when he was on the road. Kiss him goodbye, his boots crunching up the drive—eighteen wheels spitting gravel as he pulled away. Then back to bed—sheets over my head—breath hitting flannel, breathing the same air back in again. You don't deserve to drink. You don't deserve to pee... Somehow—I got up that day. I washed—put on a dress—I was even standing in the kitchen. I don't know what I was doing in there but it didn't matter... When he walked in I'd look like the woman he thought he married.

The kettle whistles; JOYCE doesn't hear it.

I asked him why the truck was still running. Is there someone else, Bill? Are you in love with someone else? He started to cry. *(Beat.)* "There's no one, Joycey. I just can't be married to you anymore." *(Gesturing to herself.)* He meant this. He couldn't stand to be around *this* anymore. Neither can I.

The kettle screams.

Scene Twelve

Courtyard. Night.

NINA stands beneath the weeping willow; branches are hitting each other in the hard, blowing wind.

NINA: Do you have it? Did you take it back? They looked everywhere—my sheets, my bed, my pillows, my shoes, my soap. *(Beat.)* I didn't look in my soap. Look, she said…see? *(She holds her ringless hand up to the sky.) "When you miss me, look at your hand. You'll see mine there. Look – see?"* I can't see your hand now. A void in a rock is me with no you. *(Beat.)* I will dig you out. I will dig I will dig, I will pull you out, my hand stronger than God, you will climb from the rock from the vug from the void you will come from the hole from the void you will come… Your ring in your hand, paper-cut sharp…will set us free.

She opens the fist of her other hand. In it is the missing piece of glass.

Scene Thirteen

Common Room. NINA enters, on her way to the kitchen. She sees JOYCE alone at the table staring at the TV, not really watching.

SAMIRA enters; it's the first time in days.

NINA: *(Beat.)* Hi.

SAMIRA: Hi.

SAMIRA sits on the couch. NINA stares into the fridge.

NINA: Cherry today. *(Beat. To SAMIRA.)* Want one?

SAMIRA: Not hungry. *(Beat. At the TV.)* What are you watching?

JOYCE: Huh? Nothing. *(Beat.)* Want me to change it?

SAMIRA: I don't care.

JOYCE gets up and turns off the television. She remains there, her back to SAMIRA.

JOYCE: *(Quietly.)* Nothing happened to me.

SAMIRA: What?

JOYCE: Nothing happened to me.

SAMIRA: *(Confused.)* When?

JOYCE: What happened to you…to Celine—to Mildred… didn't happen to me. *(Beat.)* No one did anything to me. Nothing happened to me.

Pause.

SAMIRA: It was my first apartment. I spent the whole day setting it up. I stood in front of the mirror and imagined all the parts I was going to play one day. *(Beat.)* Do you know the play *The Three Sisters* by Chekhov? He's /a playwright…

JOYCE: I'm not stupid.

SAMIRA: At the beginning, Irina says: "Why is it I'm so happy today? As if I were sailing, with the wide, blue sky above me, and great white birds soaring in the wind… I got up, I washed — and suddenly I felt everything in this world was clear to me." The minute I said those lines — a bright light blasts through the window, hits the mirror and lights me up like I really was on stage. It was just the street lamp flashing on, but that second — standing in the light looking out my window at the school I only ever dreamed of getting into — everything was clear to me too. Everything I was ever supposed to be when I was born was already me, right there in that moment. So I stopped pretending, and went to bed. *(Beat.)* I woke up in the wrong life.

Pause.

JOYCE: I don't stay in bed all day because I don't care about my life. It's the other way around. If you don't get out of bed, you can't fail at the day. *(Beat.)* I'm just… I'm just…so…

NINA: Sad.

JOYCE: Yes.

SAMIRA: Yes.

After a moment, NINA walks over to SAMIRA. She pulls the missing glass out of her left bra cup and places it on the couch beside her.

ROSEMARY enters — surprised but relieved to see SAMIRA — who immediately conceals the glass. NINA takes a seat at the table.

ROSEMARY: Hi there. *(To everyone.)* Louise is running late. She says to wait for her here.

She sits with SAMIRA on the couch.

How are you?

SAMIRA: Okay.

ROSEMARY: *(Beat.)* Al's coming tomorrow—no lawyer. If we can manage that… It's good.

SAMIRA: You don't sound too happy about it.

ROSEMARY: I'm happy. *(Beat.)* Celine left?

SAMIRA nods.

I would have liked to say goodbye.

LOUISE enters with a large folder of loose paper and art supplies — heading for the table.

LOUISE: I had big plans for today but I think we'll do some free drawing instead.

JOYCE joins LOUISE and NINA. ROSEMARY follows. LOUISE clocks SAMIRA on the couch but doesn't pressure her to join them.

LOUISE: (*Scattering the paper over the table.*) Everyone grab a sheet—there's all sizes and textures…

The women sift through them.

SAMIRA: Louise.

LOUISE: (*To the women.*) There should still be some good pieces of charcoal in that box… (*Turning to SAMIRA.*) Yes, Samira?

SAMIRA: We found this.

She holds out the piece of glass.

LOUISE stares at the glass for a moment, then puts it in her pocket.

LOUISE: (*Trying to contain her emotion.*) Everyone all set?

JOYCE: Yes.

LOUISE: Good. Let's start.

The women sketch in silence. SAMIRA watches from the couch.

ROSEMARY: (*Drawing.*) Louise?

LOUISE: Yes?

ROSEMARY: Who was that woman you were talking to?

LOUISE: *(Occupied with their work.)* What woman?

ROSEMARY: In the courtyard. I saw you from the window.

LOUISE: Oh. New girl.

The women continue working in silence.

SAMIRA walks over to the table. She picks up a piece of charcoal, then sits down and begins to draw.

End of play.